FOR JO

C000137990

JOHN O'GROATS
TO
LANDS END

THE
ULTIMATE
CHALLENGE

A WALKERS, CYCLISTS
AND MOTORISTS GUIDE

BRIAN G. SMAILES

**THERE IS A RACE TO RUN
IN ORDER TO WIN, YOU MUST
PREPARE YOURSELF TO BE
THE WINNER, NOT SIMPLY
TO DO YOUR BEST.**

Other books by the same author :-

THE LAKELAND TOP TEN
ISBN 0-9526900-3-9

THE NATIONAL 3 PEAKS WALK
ISBN 0-9526900-2-0

**THE NOVICES GUIDE TO THE
YORKSHIRE 3 PEAKS WALK**
ISBN 0-9526900-0-4

**THE NOVICES GUIDE TO THE
LYKE WAKE WALK**
ISBN 0-9526900-1-2

ISBN 0-9526900-4-7

First Published June 1999
CHALLENGE PUBLICATIONS
P.O. Box No. 132 Barnsley. S71 5YX

BRIAN SMAILES

Started his outdoor pursuits scuba diving, progressing to diving instructor. On land he initially visited an outward bound mountain school. This gave him the taste for adventure. To date he has completed 45 crossings of the 42 mile Lyke Wake Walk over the North York moors and is the record holder for the fastest 4 and 5 continuous crossings of this walk. Completing the 210 miles over rough terrain on 5 continuous crossings in June 1995, took 85 hours and 50 minutes.

His other achievements include course director for Basic Expedition Leader Award courses and author of 5 walking books.

Long distance running is one of his interests and he has completed 22 marathons and one 100km ultra run before this John O'Groats to Lands End expedition.

On water Brian has canoed the Caledonian Canal three times and the river Wye once.

Brian has travelled extensively around Great Britain and throughout Europe and in doing so has gained experience of outdoor pursuits in all conditions and weather.

Brian works on the principle of achievement through participation.

Contents

Plates

Acknowledgements

It is with grateful thanks to the following that this book has been published : -

The police and cadets from South Yorkshire Police, with particular reference to P.C. Peter West - a tireless worker who is an inspiration to us all by his commitment and enthusiasm.

Brian Huxley - Sports massage therapist.
Nigel Mitchell - Consultant dietician for the expedition.
Schoffel U K, Rutland - Gore Tex jacket.
Pulse 8 fleece clothing from B Line, Rotherham.
Pam Smailes
Nutricia - complete liquid meals (Fortisip).

Thanks also to all those who helped indirectly but who are too numerous to mention and to all who sponsored me.

JOHN O'GROATS

INVERNESS

STIRLING

CARLISLE

LANCASTER

SHREWSBURY

CHEPSTOW

BRISTOL

TAUNTON

BODMIN

LANDS END

2

Introduction

John O'Groats to Lands End is approximately 868 miles depending on which route you choose. Either way it represents a challenge that cannot be taken lightly. To enable anyone to complete this challenge requires dedication, commitment and a sense of purpose. Training for fitness, diet and training the mind are all important aspects of preparation for this ultimate   British challenge.

John O'Groats is situated at the northern tip of mainland Britain and a remote place it is. There is one hotel (currently being refurbished) a bar and a small shopping complex. Only the famous signpost stands out as the last bastion of civilisation in mainland Scotland. You can stand at the signpost with only the seabirds for company and reflect before you start on your marathon adventure, at the wisdom of it all and whether you are really sane.

The name John O'Groats dates back to 1496 and three Dutch brothers, the de Groots who worked on land and sea in that area. Because the family multiplied and built houses here, it eventually became known as John O'Groats. It overlooks the Pentland Firth which is Britain's second busiest shipping channel.

Not far away is Scapa Flow and the scuppered German fleet. This area is a divers paradise while the cliffs and distant islands are an equally special paradise for bird watchers.

Lands End in contrast is the most south westerly tip of the English mainland. Again the central point of this place is the signpost which points to John O'Groats, New York and the Isles of Scilly. Lands End is more populated than John O'Groats with a visitor centre (plate 15), food and souvenir shops. The first and last house in England is also here (plate 16). An entrance fee to gain access to Lands End visitor attractions is payable. Throughout the summer Lands End can be crowded. It covers about 100 acres and is an area of natural beauty.

The sea around Lands End is a graveyard for numerous ship wrecks, one of the more famous being the Torrey Canyon which was bombed a number of years ago to combat oil pollution.

The journey between John O'Groats and Lands End is long, tedious, undulating and picturesque. Travelling along the A9 to Inverness, then across country to the Glasgow suburbs, will take you through Stirling and the gateway from the Highlands. The main trunk roads can naturally be busy at times so care must be taken.

Journeying through northern England takes in Carlisle and Kendal on the Lake District fringe followed by Preston and Warrington in this heavily populated conurbation.

Walking to picturesque Hereford provides inspiration for any 'end to ender' knowing you are approximately 2/3 of the way through. Bristol lies ahead, then the undulating A38 towards Lands End where no doubt a warm welcome awaits you.

Read on to discover the pain and the pleasure, the highs and lows of completing the ultimate challenge -

JOHN O'GROATS to LANDS END

The Challenge

The distance is approximately 868 miles and it takes determination, careful planning and preparation to accomplish this feat.

Scotland, especially the northerly end, is remote, barren and the climate inhospitable as far as this venture is concerned. Preparations should be made to combat rain, wind, cold and equally, as you proceed south you need to prepare for heat exhaustion and sunburn.

One of the main problems on any walk is the avoidance of blisters on the feet. Severe blisters can mean the abandoning of your walk. This will be looked at further on.

Safety of any walker is essential and even more so on the narrow country lanes and dual carriageways on route. My direct experience proved that if you can attempt this walk between May and July, when there are more daylight hours, this will help. An early start if possible, 4 am, will ensure you can avoid some traffic for a few hours and be able to enjoy the wildlife and quietness around you.

There are three main sections on this walk, Scotland to the Borders, Carlisle to Bristol, then the final leg in the West country.

In the Scottish section there are a number of long ascents of up to 4 miles which seem to go on forever. One consolation is the excellent scenery including mountain ranges, valleys, lochs and pasture land. The views of the sea and cliffs both at the beginning and the end of the walk are outstanding.

My experience taught me to 'bivi' some nights and bed & breakfast (B&B) others. At least by B&B you can usually get a hot relaxing bath or a shower.

I have described to you what I consider the shortest route. In some sections you may leave a main road going off onto a side road then return later to the main road further on. These roads have been checked for distance, so don't worry if it appears initially you may be going off the beaten track. Follow the directions enclosed referring to your map if necessary.

A support team or even an individual following in a car and carrying your equipment can be a big help. Most people take between 25 - 55 days to complete this walk, so it may be difficult getting help for that length of time. Should you be able to get someone to walk with you then that will help, not just for company, but also for safety reasons.

The clothing you need, particularly your outer clothing should be appropriate for an expedition of this length and be either reflective or a light colour for safety. Reflective armbands, gloves or hood can only increase your safety.

On a walk of this length you will probably lose weight. It is important to eat regularly to keep up your energy levels (see section on food).

Now you have an insight into some of the pleasures and pains on this expedition let us continue our preparation and look at the more detailed planning.

Planning Phase

There are a number of aspects to this section so we will begin to look at each part in detail : -

The Route : -

You need to be familiar with the route well before you go. In order to do this I recommend purchasing the relevant Ordnance Survey Travelmaster maps, 5 in all. The route described herein should be drawn on the map with a highlighter pen and be learned so that you are familiar with towns, lakes, bridges or other outstanding features on the map as you go. This helps to eliminate the need to consult the map at each bend in the road on route. Try to plan a distance to walk each day. I found it helpful to walk varied distances each day, if you feel good walk as long as you feel comfortable. Some days you may not feel like it so cut down maybe to 10 or 20 miles that day.

I used a bivi bag some nights in the more remote areas and B&B's when I was near one in the evening. The advantage of a bivi bag is that it is light, waterproof and easily opened up to sleep in. Take a bin liner to put your rucksack in at night to keep it dry.

A hot bath or shower is a delight so B&B's are useful to stay in. Do not rely solely on these though because you may be in a remote area at night so a bivi bag is useful.

Clothing and Equipment : -

The months before your expedition gives you time to acquire your clothing and equipment. You may be able to get it through sponsorship from your local outdoor shop. There is a vast array of equipment available. Whatever you buy it needs to be strong and durable enough to last the length of your expedition.

Your outer garments i.e. jacket and trousers, ideally need to be waterproof and breathable. Above all, your clothing needs to keep you warm and protect you from the elements. Any jacket or equipment you buy should either be a light colour or have reflective stripes on it for safety (plate 1).

Your rucksack needs to be large enough to get all your belongings in. The size will depend on whether you are being supported on your walk or not and whether you intend to camp, use a bivi bag or B&B on route. I used a large rucksack and limited my belongings to only the necessary essentials. Every kilogram mounts up and it is a long way to carry even a light rucksack.

You need a torch but don't take one that needs four or six large batteries, think of the weight. One of the small type with a halogen bulb is excellent and light to carry.

Your footwear is probably the most important item. Suffer problems with your feet and you may need to abandon your walk. Select a pair of boots well before you go and get assistance with fitting so they are comfortable. Some people like leather boots, others fabric. Whatever you choose wear them regularly for walks and at other times so they are properly bedded in before you go. Along with your boots I suggest taking a pair of trainers, should you experience problems then change into trainers for a while. This spreads the pressure on your feet by alternating footwear.

One further important item of footwear is the addition of sorbothane innersoles. These help to cushion your feet as the walking is mostly on roads. The innersoles cost around £15-£18 and are well worth the expense.

Food : -

Any food you take should if possible be dehydrated to lighten your load. I found an extremely useful addition was complete meals in liquid form. This often eliminates the need for cooking on route. You get all the vitamins, protein and carbohydrate you need with these meals so it is worth purchasing some.

Planning your route carefully can mean you arrive near a village at meal times. Cafes, restaurants and bar meals maybe available, I used these often. A ready cooked hot meal will give you energy to continue the next section. Using the villages and towns to buy hot food or liquid meals and to replenish your rucksack stock can mean you do not need to take a cooking stove with you. I did not take a stove and I managed adequately without one.

Try to get one hot meal each day, using liquid complete meals at other times. Supplement your diet with fruit, chocolate etc. as required.

Training Plan

To complete a venture as long as this, requires a high level of fitness and stamina. You need to start your training early. A six month programme should be enough to get you to peak fitness. Start your training with short walks then over the six months increase your distance up to 30 miles a day. Practice walking with a rucksack and gradually increase the weight so you become accustomed to carrying a heavy pack. This is important as the shoulders can ache a lot.

You may find that any extra training you can do in the gym would be helpful. Use weights to strengthen legs and shoulders. Any jogging you can do will help to increase stamina. Assuming you can jog 10 miles on a running machine in the gym or around your neighbourhood then you should find walking 20 miles easier.

Plan a programme up to your expedition, incorporating walking, jogging and weight training/gym work if possible. Finally experiment using complete liquid meals and wear all your walking equipment when training. Simulate as near as possible in training the conditions you will encounter on your expedition. It is by doing this that you will be prepared for the real thing.

Practical Advice

The checklist below is a summary of some of the essential points you need to consider :-

1. Ensure you can understand and read a map sufficiently before you start.

2. Ensure the maps are up to date showing current roads. Study maps thoroughly beforehand.

3. Try to plan your night stops near villages/towns using campsites or B&B's.

4. Plan a training programme, gradually increasing distance and upper body strength.

5. Rucksack and outer clothing should be bright with reflective stripes on them if possible.

6. Ensure boots are properly 'bedded in'.

7. Take plenty of socks and a pair of trainers. Change socks and footwear around frequently.

8. Take a good supply of blister treatments and treat blisters promptly.

9. Ensure all food, clothing and other items carried are kept to a minimum.

10. Have someone to meet you periodically, if possible with changes of clothes, food etc.

11. Use every opportunity to replenish food and drink stocks in each village.

12. Take a supply of energy bars and plenty of liquid for frequent daily consumption.

13. Alternate between bivi bag and B&B if possible.

14. Get an early start at 4am if possible. This may be difficult in B&B's.

15. Walk on footpaths if possible or on grass verges. Only walk on roads if absolutely necessary.

16. Be aware of traffic at all times.

17. Should you need publicity for your sponsors, then inform your local radio, T.V. stations and local newspapers giving them full details.

18. Keep details on your person of next of kin, medical information, blood group etc. in case of accident or emergency.

19. Register at John O'Groats Hotel or the last house. Check in at Lands End.

Publicity and Sponsorship

In any event like this it is not just the challenge of completing the event but to raise sponsor money for a worthwhile cause. There are a number of ways you can do this. One way is to produce sponsor forms well in advance. These can be sponsored per mile or any other distance.

An alternative to the well used sponsor form is guess your finishing time tickets. These are similar to raffle tickets but the person sponsoring has to guess the time in days, hours, minutes and seconds you will take to complete your walk. It is pure guess work. You could donate a cash or other prize to the winner. This is a good method of raising money but check your local council regarding a lottery licence.

Another method is to ask companies for a sizeable donation if you are prepared to display a sign on your support vehicle advertising their business. I have used this method along with the others mentioned and had good results with each one. You may find that some companies will be pleased to offer walking equipment in return for advertising on a support vehicle if you have one.

With sponsorship, as with any other task, the harder you try to raise money the more you can raise.

Publicity is essential, especially in your local area. Any unusual method of travelling between the two points may warrant extra publicity in national newspapers, walking magazines or on T.V. Local radio stations could be contacted with a mobile phone on route if you can collect all the telephone numbers before you go. Telephone them well before you get into their area to enable them to plan and make arrangements to contact you on route for a live interview if they need one.

Finally sponsorship will not only help you in raising money for charities, but can provide equipment for you to ease the financial burden, even to the extent of supplying fuel for a support vehicle. I have found it gives you encouragement to walk when you know that so many people have sponsored you and are relying on your fitness, willpower and motivation to get you to the finish.

You may find you can even get blister treatments or complete liquid meals sponsored by chemist shops.

One final word on publicity/sponsorship. You can be as successful as your imagination and determination to succeed will allow you. Think hard on how much you need to raise and what clothing, equipment or fuel you can get sponsored, then set about your task with enthusiasm.

Financial Considerations

A challenge such as this can, if you do not plan it properly, make a sizeable hole in your pocket. Initially you need to purchase your main equipment, clothing, rucksack, boots, maps etc. These alone can cost a lot of money if you cannot get them sponsored.

Once you have your equipment you need to plan how to get from your home to John O'Groats. Haulage companies have a network of contacts to help, so make enquiries with them early. I used this method, with an occasional lift in a car in the more remote parts of the route to John O'Groats.

On enquiring about trains and buses, I found they either did not connect in Inverness or did not venture further north from Inverness at night. Travelling costs by train was high, whereby coach fares were about half the price. This cost can be eliminated if you can arrange any lifts with haulage companies at least to Inverness or Wick.

Probably your biggest cost will be for B&B's if you use them. Between John O'Groats and Inverness they start from £10 and rise to £25 per night in some but generally expect to pay £15 per night for B&B with a bath or shower included. Plan your stops as near as possible to villages where you would expect to find B&B's but carry a tent or bivi bag either for alternate nights or if there is no B&B in the area.

Using a bivi bag or even a small tent overnight in a field will probably be free if you stop late and rise early. Ask permission from farms etc. where necessary. My preferred method is alternating between bivi bag and B&B's which worked very well enabling me to have a hot bath/shower every other night but keeping costs down.

Feeding a support team and purchasing fuel can be expensive, so it may be better to arrange for someone to meet you every 6 days with a supply of clothes and food etc. rather than stay throughout the expedition.

Food for the expedition may cost slightly more but you would eat at home anyway so it is not a large cost. You will find that complete liquid meals can be a big help if you are not near a village for a bar meal, fish and chips or other food. These give all nourishment the body needs and are not large quantities to digest. They cost about £3.00 each but shop around.

The above is a résumé of the main costs but produce your own accounting sheet while giving consideration to the above points.

Support Team

Over two thousand people a year attempt this challenge. Many walk unsupported, others with full or partial support. Due to the distance involved and the time element, it may be a problem to get an individual or a team to give continued support throughout the expedition.

I have already given details of what I consider the best method of travelling with support meeting you every 6 days. This way you can get clean clothes and fresh supplies brought to you. It is not essential to do this and you can be self sufficient for the entire journey. You will of course have clothes, socks etc. to wash on route. Drying them may be a problem.

Those of you who have a support team whether they are using a car or a mini bus, need to ask yourselves the following questions :-

1. How many people do you effectively need to give adequate support. More people means more food to provide. This increases overall costs.

2. What sleeping arrangements do you have for all the support team. Will they be camping, B&B or in the back of a van for the night. Will you be incurring accommodation charges.

3. What type of vehicle will a support team use. Will it be road worthy for this type of journey. Your vehicle should not be a thirsty one. A diesel vehicle may be more economical.

4. Have you enough room in the vehicle for everyone. It is a long way and can take a long time, so the support team needs room to put all equipment away safely and still have room to move inside the vehicle.

5. Are the support team equipped and trained to cope with map reading, long days driving and first aid, including blister treatment.

6. Washing and drying everyone's clothes may be a problem, especially in the remote areas of Scotland. Therefore, you will need to take soap powder etc.

Careful planning and consideration of the above points means that you are prepared for the long, tedious journey ahead and you have done your best to ensure that the support team provides an adequate service.

When deciding how many support team members you need, I would suggest three people. All should be able to drive and navigate. They should also walk with you on a rota basis to keep you company for some stretches of the route.

You may be fortunate to get three people to accompany you but it is not essential. Which ever way you elect to plan your journey, take an objective look at the overall task and consider carefully the different options. Ultimately it could mean the success or failure of the expedition.

Synopsis of the Route

John O'Groats can be a bleak, windswept and remote place to start your expedition. When you leave, the first section consists of a two way road with a slight climb to the first village to join the A99. It is usually windy in this area most of the time.

When you walk on the undulating road towards Wick you pass through some small villages. Some consist of only a few isolated houses or farmsteads. Progressing further you will find more shops and houses as you go south. Wick is a main town in this area for rest, refreshments and food etc.

Following the route from Wick you continue on the coast road south. There are a number of large ascents and descents here. Further down the coast Brora and Golspie are decent sized villages where you can get food and other items. As you continue south there are long bridges to cross. The bridge over the Cromarty Firth is the longest followed by a long climb up the south side onto the Black Isle. Just before Inverness you again cross an impressive bridge over the Moray Firth. The road for the past 30 miles has been mostly dual carriageways. These can be busy at peak times particularly as you approach Inverness and beyond.

Leaving Inverness there is a long climb past Culloden followed by undulating dual carriageway. Continue past Slochd summit then Aviemore and Dalwhinnie all on dual carriageways. The scenery and remoteness are awe inspiring since leaving John O'Groats.

Pass through Glen Garry before turning off right to Trinafour and a long downhill stretch to Tummel Bridge. Continue on these back roads to Crieff. The roads from Glen Garry are undulating and narrow so take care and wear bright clothes. You approach Dunblane and a busier section through Stirling, Denny, Cumbernauld and Airdrie. The route turns rural as you go south towards Gretna and the Borders.

Pass through Lockerbie and on to Gretna. The route is gradually getting busier as you walk parallel with the M74 towards Carlisle. Walk on the A6 to Penrith where the route over Shap Fell to Kendal becomes hilly and less inhabited than previously. Walking towards Lancaster you are approaching a town with full amenities and a large population. The route continues for the most part to be extremely busy as you walk through Preston, Wigan and Warrington. The hardest thing about walking this section between Preston and south of Warrington is following the roads which is difficult through these towns and built up areas. Follow my directions and a map closely.

Should you think it beneficial then purchase a town map of Preston, Wigan and Warrington. I found it difficult to travel through this area. An alternative would be to have a test run in a car beforehand to find your way through the maze.

You now reach the A49 at Stockton Heath. From here it is easier travelling towards Whitchurch and through all the small villages on route. Whitchurch has a by-pass then you come to Shrewsbury still on the A49 towards Ludlow. All the roads from Warrington to Chepstow are two way roads so utmost care must be taken. Travel through Hereford to Monmouth. This is a nice town. I stayed here on my expedition.

Continue to Chepstow past the racecourse and over the Severn Bridge (there is no charge going east). The views are impressive walking over the bridge. The next section through Bristol and west on the A38 is another part where you need to refer closely to my route and possibly a town map. Your route passes under the Clifton Suspension Bridge, so that may help you with your navigation here.

Once on the south west side of Bristol continue on dual carriageway and two way roads to Bridgewater. Passing through Bridgewater you walk to Taunton where you can again walk directly through the town to the south west side still on the A38 to Tiverton. Many of these roads are narrow and winding so take utmost care.

Pass through Tiverton on route to Okehampton then to Launceston. The rolling hills and valleys command all your energy now as you probably have blisters on blisters and are well past your best by this time.

The A30 you walk on takes you over Bodmin Moor then through Bodmin on the A389 to rejoin the A30 and by-pass Redruth on the dual carriageway.

Penzance is ahead and you see St. Michael's Mount off to your left. Leave the roundabout that leads to Penzance and you are on the last leg of your journey to Lands End. Then celebrate when you get there. You have achieved your goal.

Many people travel from Lands End to John O'Groats. It is often said that you travel with the prevailing wind this way. After due consideration I opted to walk from John O'Groats to Lands End. There are two main reasons for this decision :-

1. I find it better to start in a more mountainous and windy or generally colder area when I am fit and my energy levels are high, progressing to a warmer area as I proceed south. Walking this direction means the mountains and the more remote sections of Scotland are tackled earlier rather than later.

2. The fact that the prevailing wind is westerly or south westerly should not make a difference because walking is generally slow. It would make a difference however if I was jogging or cycling.

Safety Considerations

Much of this route consists of walking on roads which can be extremely busy especially with rush hour traffic. It is very important to be aware of the hazards a walker poses to the unsuspecting driver. I resolved that an early start at 4am or just before dawn helped me to cover a good distance before a lot of traffic and petrol fumes polluted the roads and atmosphere.

Throughout the route there are footpaths particularly in or near villages. Use these wherever possible. Large sections of the route are along dual carriageways. Usually there are grass verges where you can walk safely alongside the road. When dark this presents a problem so you need a good torch.

Walking on roads with no footpaths or grass verges can be extremely dangerous if you are not constantly observing the traffic. In situations like this you should walk facing oncoming traffic keeping close to the side of the road. A most important point is to wear light coloured or reflective outer clothing (plate 1). You can buy reflective strips to stitch onto your rucksack, jacket and trousers. A yellow jacket or hat helps motorists to see you and may prevent an accident happening.

Plate 1
The Signpost at Lands End

The above points and dangers cannot be stressed too strongly. Follow the highway code, see and be seen at all times. You cannot let your attention wander when you are walking on roads with no footpaths or verge.

Carry an identity tag or card in case of accident and contact friends and relatives regularly to report your position.

Another safety consideration would be to have a good supply of first aid items. On this type of venture you will probably need more blister kits and dressings for your feet. A plentiful supply of adhesive plasters are recommended as is foot powder and lip balm.

Depending on the time of year you may need midge cream/spray and sun cream. Sunglasses may be of benefit in mid summer. It is important not to dehydrate so a good supply of water or other drinks is recommended. Drink frequently and refill at each available point you can especially if you sweat a lot while walking.

Summarising this section, I would say the two most important points to consider are wearing light coloured and reflective clothing and having plenty of liquid to avoid dehydration.

The Countdown

The training is now complete and you are ready to pack your equipment. You should already have a checklist which you have made over the past two months. Hopefully you have had some practice walks with all your equipment on. Almost certainly your pack will be very heavy. Are the straps on the rucksack strong enough for the journey? Can you get all your clothing and equipment packed comfortably and is it inside a waterproof bag?

Your boots should be well walked in by now and the leather soft and supple. During the final week before you go you should cut right down on your training to build up and store energy and give your body a chance to recover from any minor strains and sprains. Check all equipment thoroughly and study your maps again. Don't forget the weather report for the week ahead before you leave.

Your local newspaper may want a photograph and a report before you leave. This may help your sponsorship drive. You may like to collect and save any newspaper reports to reflect on after the event. It is a good idea to contact any major sponsors of your equipment to give them last minute reports before you set off.

Should you be taking a support team, then make sure you have made the correct insurance arrangements for the drivers of the vehicle. Have you made arrangements for purchasing fuel either by cash or credit card. Some of the large supermarkets and filling stations can provide you with a list of all their outlets throughout the country. Northern Scotland tends to have fewer filling stations but it should not be too much of a problem the further south you go.

You will find a good supply of energy drinks, energy bars and glucose based sweets can help you to maintain a constant supply of energy while walking.

Before you leave have a good nights sleep. Wherever you start from in the U.K. you will probably find there are good transport links to Scotland. Once you reach Stirling it may be harder to catch coach connections and especially once you reach Inverness. Depending on the time you arrive in Inverness you may find that both buses and trains have stopped for the day, so check it out first if using public transport. Trains stop at Wick and you need a local bus connection if you can get one from Wick to John O'Groats. I used a haulage company to get to Inverness and arranged lifts from there to John O'Groats arriving at 4.30pm and ready for a 4am start the next day.

In John O'Groats there are numerous B&B's but you cannot really get a 4am start when staying in one of these. There is a good campsite and you can of course camp/bivi there as I did. Showers and toilets are available. There is a hotel (currently being refurbished) and a bar and café to purchase meals. You need to register either in the bar of the John O'Groats hotel or in the gift shop known as 'The Last House in Scotland'. Complete the form, get it stamped or signed and take it with you to Lands End.

The day has finally arrived and you are in John O'Groats, the official start line is outside the John O'Groats hotel near the large car park. After the customary photograph you are off on your adventure of a lifetime!

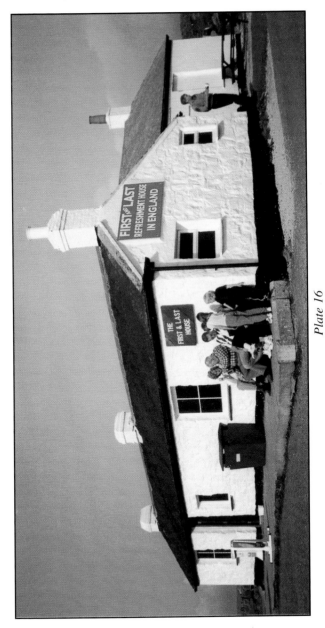

Plate 16
You left the Last House in Scotland to walk to the Last House in England.

Pre - Route Information

The following route is not written in specific mileage sections in order to describe the route better in difficult areas. It may appear descriptive in towns or built up areas, then cover a long distance over one page.

Grid references and compass bearings have not been used as all your route is on roads. Carefully follow the route stated and where necessary refer to your map. Road numbers and town/village names should be enough, together with a basic knowledge of maps to get any walker from John O'Groats to Lands End successfully.

The Route in Detail

In John O'Groats there is a hotel (currently being refurbished), with the famous signpost nearby. This is similar to the Lands End signpost and an ideal point for a photograph before leaving. There is a large car park and over spill car parks surrounding the small shopping area. This consists of a tourist information centre, a café, gift shops and the last house in Scotland (plate 2). A good campsite is nearby with full amenities.

A ferry service runs to the Orkney Islands from John O'Groats. There are good views looking towards the islands and the busy shipping lane between the mainland and the islands.

Your starting point, after you have registered in the hotel or the last house gift shop, is the white line across the car parking area outside the John O'Groats hotel. Leave John O'Groats on the 'B' road walking slightly uphill past the B&B's. Looking back there are fine views of the islands and of Duncansby Head to your left. Walk to the main A99 road, then follow the sign to Wick. Carry on slightly uphill on the metalled road, over the brow of the hill, followed by a long gradual decent. The surrounding area is moorland. You probably have at least a gentle breeze if not stronger here.

Plate 2
The Author emerging from the Last House in Scotland after registration.

Plate 3
One of the steep ascent and decents between Dunbeath and Helmsdale.

You arrive at Freswick after 3 miles which consists of a number of isolated houses and farms, together with some B&B's, starting from £10.00. Just past Freswick there are good views of Noss Head and Brough Head looking seaward.

Next you pass through Auckengill, again with isolated houses, one fuel station and the Northlands Viking Centre tourist attraction. An excellent view of Noss Head is off to your left. Your route takes you through Keiss on a long straight road with mountains in the distance beyond. Sinclairs Bay offers excellent views to your left. The road becomes busier at Reiss as you follow the sign to Wick. There are more houses here but no shops since you left John O' Groats.

Entering Wick you pass Caithness Glass Visitors Centre on your left. Wick is a small town with a full range of shops, restaurants etc. A hospital is also situated here. Continue over the bridge through Wick and through the traffic lights on the south side. Leaving the town you pass the football ground and cemetery on your left. Continue on the A99 through Thrumster passing the caravan site and T.V./radio masts. Next village is Ulbster, again a small collection of isolated houses and crofts. Walking past Halberry Head you have good views of the mountains ahead as you approach them.

Your next village is Occumster, there is a lot of sheep and cattle farming here on moorland with isolated farms on the hillsides.

You arrive at Lybster which has hotels, B&B's, tourist information and food available. Passing through Latheron there is a telephone box, garage and some houses. At Latheronwheel village there is camping at the side of the hotel. The facilities are good and reasonably priced. Leaving Latheronwheel there is a steep decent, then a gradual climb up the other side.

Next town is Dunbeath where camping is available. Dunbeath Castle stands impressive as a white painted building on the cliffs. Cross the bridge and ascend the hill as you leave. The road winds around the cliffs towards Helmsdale. There are footpaths to walk on rather than roads as you pass through the villages. You pass a fuel station which sells confectionery.

Berriedale is the next village and there is another steep winding road descending then ascending. You can see your route well in front of you. There is a post office at the bottom of the hill. The ascent is 0.8 of a mile and there is a forest on your right hand side as you leave the village (plate 3).

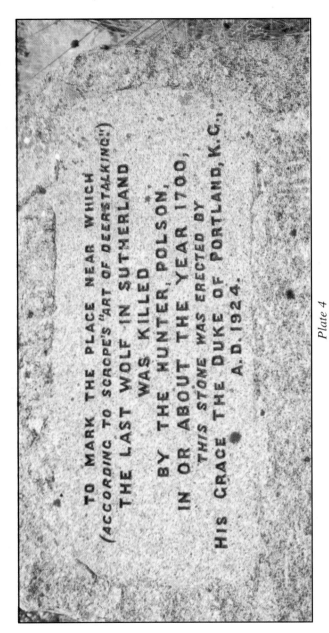

Plate 4
The plaque near Loth describing an historic event.

TO MARK THE PLACE NEAR WHICH
(ACCORDING TO SCROPE'S "ART OF DEERSTALKING")
THE LAST WOLF IN SUTHERLAND
WAS KILLED
BY THE HUNTER, POLSON,
IN OR ABOUT THE YEAR 1700,
THIS STONE WAS ERECTED BY
HIS GRACE THE DUKE OF PORTLAND, K.C.,
A.D. 1924.

40

Before you arrive at Helmsdale there are some long gradual descents and a long ascent before the sharp hairpin bends which start about one mile before Helmsdale with a final steep descent into the village. There are B&B's on your right, shops and a harbour in this small village. Just across the small bridge in Helmsdale is a tourist information centre with a campsite nearby.

The footpath which leads out of Helmsdale stops outside of the village. The railway runs parallel to the undulating road which has numerous bends as it hugs the shoreline going south towards Portgower. Portgower consists of a telephone box and a small collection of houses on the hillside.

Walk through Loth village which is similar to the last, apart from the lay-by just beyond. Here you will find the memorial denoting the last wolf in Sutherland which was killed there (plate 4). The road now is undulating and you can see the point of Brora village. There are two campsites as you reach Brora. The long main street and shops at the far end enable you to replenish your food supply.

There are numerous bends as you continue to Golspie but take care as there are no footpaths to walk on. As you approach Golspie there is an excellent view of the bay and Dunrobin Castle.

There is a railway station and some small shops in Golspie's long narrow village. You can purchase most items needed for your journey here. Leaving Golspie you may see a statue on top of the hill.

Loch Fleet bridge is your next desination and the road is quite flat towards Dornoch. You should go over an area called 'The Mound' which takes you down by the estuary. After crossing Loch Fleet ascend gradually before descending again to by-pass Dornoch. There are a number of campsites in this village which is 2.5 miles off the main A9 road. Commercial forestry is evident all around this area. There are two telephone boxes on the A9 near Dornoch.

Passing a fuel station on the A9 near Dornoch, a sharp right hand bend takes you to the long bridge over the Dornock Firth near Tain. As you approach the bridge you may see the village of Tain and the white chimney of the Glenmorangie distillery just off the A9. There are excellent views in all directions while crossing the bridge. Keep to the footpath over the bridge as the wind can be very strong in this area.

On reaching the roundabout on the south side, turn right off the A9 onto a shorter route along the A836 for 2.8 miles to Edderton. There is a forest on your left and some trees on your right side.

Go past a caravan sales centre then turn left to Aultnamain at the war memorial. The route ascends up a narrow road with good scenery which gets even better as you proceed. After climbing initially the road becomes generally flat for 1.5 miles before you reach the main B9176 which was the old A9 road. Turn left at the junction and continue over a number of cattle grids. There is a lot of forestry here but the views are good in all directions.

Approaching Alness you have good views of the Cromarty Firth ahead before a gradual descent to rejoin the A9 near Alness. The services situated at the A9 junction can be recommended for a good cheap meal. Turn right and continue along the dual carriageway, walking along the grass verge of this busy road. Nearing the bridge over the Cromarty Firth on the A9 you will see your route ascending on the Black Isle to your left. The wind can be extremely strong as you leave the roundabout and cross the bridge which is 1.1 miles long. There is a climb of 3.6 miles on dual carriageway before a long descent to a roundabout at Tore.

Your next section is an extremely busy dual carriageway from Tore roundabout to Inverness. It can be hard walking on the grass but necessary for your safety. Before you arrive at Inverness you pass North Kessock and Charlestown.

There are some B&B's and camping situated at the bottom of the main street at Charlestown about 0.5 of a mile from the A9. You arrive soon at an impressive bridge over the Moray Firth estuary. The views are excellent as you walk on the path to the roundabout on the south side. The large town of Inverness starts here should you want to stay or replenish your supplies.

You pass Caledonian Thistle football ground near this roundabout and the dual carriageway continues towards Aviemore. There is no footpath so walk on the grass again. There is a 3 mile gradual ascent on which you pass the turn off to the battlefield of Culloden. Continue on the A9 passing a tourist information centre on your right as you go over the brow of the hill.

Cross over the river Nairn and there is a campsite at Moy near Moy Hall. There are a number of long ascents and descents with forest and moorland on both sides of the road. Eventually you pass Tomatin services, which is a good refreshment stop. Crossing a bridge over the river Findhorn, you ascend slightly up to Slochd summit with excellent views all around. This section is a two-way road so take care, walking on the grass as much as possible. The road has snow poles at each side as you leave Slochd summit to denote the road in winter.

Plate 5
Walking towards Trinafour with Loch Con in the background.

Pass a turn off to Carrbridge on your left. Should you need food or shelter the village is 2 miles further on. Aviemore is the next main turn off that you pass on the A9. Continue on the main road which is both dual carriageway and two-way. Walk past the turn off to Dalwhinnie, where the railway runs parallel with the road.

Drumochter summit is a short distance from Dalwhinnie. A plaque at the side depicts an historic battle. This section is a long stretch of dual carriageway. You turn right on Drumochter Pass towards Trinafour off the A9. This single track road winds around and over a hill and there are good views in all directions. There is a dam on your right side with Loch Con behind it (plate 5). You can see your route ahead as you go around a hairpin bend.

The next loch you pass is Loch Errochty, just before Trinafour. You come to a T-junction, take the right turn B847 towards Aberfeldy and Kinloch Rannock. After 0.75 of a mile turn off left to Tummel Bridge ascending the metalled one track road. Once you reach the brow of the hill there is a very long walk down the other side past Tay Forest Park to Tummel Bridge. At the T-junction at the bottom turn left on the B846 and go over Tummel Bridge following signs to Aberfeldy. Go past a clean, new power station at the side of Loch Tummel river.

You pass Loch Kinadockie, a small loch after Tummel Bridge. The road is undulating with a lot of downhill sections. Passing a deer park, go downhill and take the second turn off right towards Kenmore. Go over the bridge alongside Loch Tay. Turn onto the road to Amulree along the Glen Quaich road. At Amulree turn right on the A822 to Crieff. The scenery is good all around this area. After a downhill section there is a picnic area by the side of the river in Sma Glen.

Follow the A85 now to Crieff. Go straight through the centre of Crieff to the T-junction, then turn left to Stirling on the A822 again. Crieff is a pleasant town with plenty of shops and worth a stop on your expedition.

Walk along the main A822 road through Muthill. Stay on this road to join the A9 towards Dunblane. You arrive at a village called Braco then rejoin the A9 2 miles after Braco. This section is usually busy dual carriageway, so take extreme care.

The shortest route is through Dunblane, so turn left at the first turning marked Dunblane and Kinbuck on the B8033. In Dunblane follow the B8033 to Stirling at the roundabout. This part is dual carriageway. You come to another roundabout at the other side of Dunblane signposted Bridge of Allan.

Follow this road through Bridge of Allan. A sign points right to Stirling and to a campsite (avoiding low bridge). Turn right here, you pass the campsite.

Continue towards Stirling on this road then onto a dual carriageway that skirts around Stirling. Go through an underpass towards St. Ninians then Denny on the A872. You come to a roundabout. Take the A9 to St. Ninians. There is a footpath on this section. Walk through the built up area known as St. Ninians. You pass Bannockburn Heritage Centre on your right. A sign states Stirling services ½ mile. You come to a large roundabout as you leave the built up area. Follow the sign to Denny on the A872. This roundabout takes you over the motorway. A campsite is 1 mile along this road. The A872 runs parallel with the motorway to Denny. There is a footpath along this road.

You arrive at a village called Dunipace but continue on the A872. At the T-junction turn right following A803 towards Glasgow. A mini roundabout is signposted A80. Continue on this road then bear right to Haggs. Another mini roundabout marked Glasgow A80/M80 is to your right here. Follow this onto the A80 dual carriageway. A sign states Carlisle 100 miles. Take care when walking, using the grass verge as much as possible. Turn off to Cumbernauld on the A8011 when you see the sign which is opposite a fuel station.

Arriving at Cumbernauld, keep on the dual carriageway to a sign saying Carlisle A73. Take this road to another dual carriageway which descends. Another sign says Airdrie A73, take this road. Be aware of the dangers on the roads at all times in this heavily populated area. Turn left at the next three roundabouts marked Carlisle and Airdrie. You come to a slip road which you stay on towards Airdrie. At the next roundabout follow A73 straight to Airdrie.

Once you arrive at Airdrie continue to a roundabout then follow the signs to Lanark A73 south. At the next roundabout continue on the A73 to Lanark. You pass the Airdrieonians football club on your left. Continue through an area known as Chapelhall. A sign at a large roundabout states Glasgow M80 and Edinburgh A80. The road soon divides but keep on the A73 towards Peebles. Another roundabout has a war memorial on it. Follow A73 to Peebles off to your right. Go across another roundabout with traffic lights marked Lanark A73. Cross a mini roundabout following Lanark signs. Leaving Carluke there are good views over open countryside going south.

Walk into Lanark following signs to Carlisle A73. Pass the railway station on your left in the main high street. At the T-junction turn left following Carlisle A73. Leaving Lanark there is a nice picnic area at Lanark Moor Country Park which you walk past on your left. Leave Lanark on A73 until you meet the A70 leading towards the M74 at Uddington. Cross the river Clyde where it is signposted A70 to Ayr. Do not take this road but turn left on the A73 which is a long straight road. Follow this road until it joins the A702 signposted Carlisle and Abington.

Walk through the small community of Roberton where there are B&B's and a telephone box. Arriving at junction 13 roundabout at the M74, turn left on the A702 to Crawford. This road runs parallel with the M74. Continue on this road, following signs to Crawford local services, into the village. There is camping and B&B's here. Now follow sign for Beattock B7076. There may be roadworks/motorway construction, so take care for the next 20 miles south. This road joins the A74 (road may be re-numbered after roadworks are complete). Continue on this road which runs parallel to the new section of motorway.

Turn left off the A74 to Johnstonebridge on the B7076 taking you under the M74 motorway then turning left again following signs to Lockerbie. There are services at this point. Your road again runs parallel with the motorway. Turn off at the roundabout just before your walk into Lockerbie. Follow the signs to Annan B723 then to Gretna Green. Follow the next signs for the B7076 to Ecclefechan, where camping is available. Continue through the village. Your route winds under the motorway then runs parallel with it towards Kirtlebridge and Gretna Green. The road passes over the A74M. You by-pass the small village of Kirtlebridge and go through the village of Kirkpatrick Fleming. There is a campsite in this village.

Follow the signs from Kirkpatrick Fleming to Gretna Green (plate 6). The old smithy is in Gretna Green along with B&B's. Walk into the village then turn right following a sign saying 'all routes', turn left on a local road to Carlisle B7076. Walking through Gretna village past some B&B's, you pass a sign saying 'Welcome to England'. Cross the bridge then take Longtown A6071. Once you arrive in Longtown turn right on the A7 to Carlisle. This section is 3 miles longer by going to Longtown but the A74 road between Gretna and junction 44 of the M6 is considered to be too dangerous to walk along.

Plate 6
A milestone on your expedition, the famous Gretna Green.

Walk into Carlisle on the A7 following city centre signs. Look for signs A6 Penrith. Turn off left to Penrith, do not go into Carlilse city centre. Pick up the A6 which runs parallel with the motorway soon after leaving Carlisle. This takes you into Penrith and beyond. There are many B&B's in the Carlisle area. There is a footpath as you leave Carlisle towards Penrith. At a roundabout follow A6 Penrith right into Penrith. At the one way system continue along the main street through the shopping area in a direct line through the town. You come to a roundabout signposted Shap A6, take this route.

Walk to Eamont Bridge on the A6, passing Lowther holiday park on your right. Continue on the winding road to Shap, through the village of Clifton, then over the M6. You go through Hackthorpe village, cross over the M6, then under it on to Shap village. There are B&B's in Shap. Walk over Shap summit on the A6 at 1400ft. Continue on A6 to Kendal. Walk straight through Kendal centre and pick up the A591/A6 to Lancaster again. A footpath runs right through Kendal and out on the south side. The road is signposted Lancaster A591 at a roundabout and section of dual carriageway with a footpath.

You arrive at junction 36 of the M6, go across then turn off on the A6070 to Holme Burton.

The M6 is now on your right as you walk towards Lancaster. Follow signs towards Burton going over the M6 again. Approaching Burton in Kendal you may see the church on the rise in front of you with a weather vane on top. Continue through the village to a roundabout signposted Lancaster A6. At a large roundabout follow signs for Carnforth. There is camping here as you go through the village. There are a further two campsites as you continue towards the village of Bolton le Sands on route to Lancaster.

Arriving in Lancaster follow the one way system towards the town centre then past the university campus. At the south end of the town there is a roundabout signed A6 south, passing a university building and park area on your left. A footpath leads out of Lancaster for a long way. The M6 is on your left. Walk through the village of Galgate and over the Lancaster canal. At a roundabout follow A6 to Preston. Keep on the footpath. Next village is Scorton. Bear right at a fork in the road to Preston.

Walking into Garstang, continue through the traffic lights to Preston, walking through Catterall then Bilsborrow and Barton. There are B&B's here as you pass. After Barton you come to a roundabout under the M55.

Go straight across on the A6 to Preston. Continue through the traffic lights to Fulwood then through another two sets. Preston park and football ground are on your left as you walk towards the town centre. Continue on the A6 towards Chorley. Bear left at a fork in the road towards Chorley/Manchester A6. Pass Sainsburys homebase store on your right. Turn right at a fork to Chorley on a dual carriageway section. Follow signs at next two roundabouts to Chorley.

At the next roundabout turn left, passing a Sainsburys fuel station. At the next lights follow Euxton A49 to your right. Walk under the M6 on a footpath. The M6 is now on your right as you walk along this tree lined road. Walk across the traffic lights on the A49 while approaching the outskirts of Leyland, passing a golf club on your left. Follow the sign now to Wigan A49. Go across a mini roundabout then an uphill climb leads into open countryside. Next place to pass through is Coppull then Standish village.

Arriving at the traffic lights in Standish continue on the A49 towards Wigan. There is a footpath all the way. Turn right at a mini roundabout then when you enter Wigan walk straight through the town centre rather than on the ring road. Follow the A49 in a straight line to Warrington. Your route takes you down the side of Wigan rugby club.

Walk alongside three multi storey car parks on the A49, through the underpass then turn left on the A49 to Warrington. Your route takes you along the side of a canal on your left. At a roundabout turn left to Warrington. Turn left at the next roundabout following Ashton A49. There is a park on your right. Turn right at traffic lights then cross the next set of lights walking out of Wigan.

Proceed past Haydock racecourse on your left, then turn left at a large roundabout under the M6, marked Newton A49. Arriving at a T-junction, turn left onto the A49 and under a railway arch as you leave Newton le Willows.

Approaching a large roundabout walk across towards Warrington town centre. Pass a retail park on your right then cross another roundabout towards Warrington. Follow Warrington/Whitchurch signs. The route takes you over Warrington new bridge. Cross a busy junction with traffic lights following Whitchurch A49. The route now is straightforward and takes you over another bridge.

The A49 to Whitchurch bears off to the left in front of the church, passing Greenalls brewery on the right. Continue through more traffic lights and over another bridge across the Manchester ship canal. You have now left the main Warrington area and you enter Stockton Heath.

Plate 7
Passing through Whitchurch over halfway on your expedition.

Cross a set of traffic lights walking along a tree lined road. At the next small roundabout go straight across on London Road. You enter Stretton village. Continue through another set of traffic lights beside the Cat and Lion pub. At junction 10 of the M56 take the A49 Whitchurch road. Walk over the next traffic lights to Whitchurch passing over a canal at Bartington. Turn right to Whitchurch at a roundabout on the A49 then go through Cuddington. Continue through three sets of lights. There is more open country here and not many B&B's or camping sites available. Turn right at a pub called the Red Fox. Pass over a canal then go through Spurston village. Accommodation is available at the Charmondley Arms on the A49 near Whitchurch. Leave the A49 when you get to the town centre (plate 7).

There are two mini roundabouts where you turn left at both to take you into Whitchurch town centre. Do not follow the ring road. Follow signs to B5476 Wem at a mini roundabout at the south end of the town centre. Pass the Whitchurch ambulance station on your right and keep on the B5476 to Wem which is the most direct route. Walk to a T-junction near Wem town centre, turn right towards Shrewsbury. Turn left by the church still on the B5476. Pass the Bridgewater Arms pub on your right. The roads are quite flat in this area. Walk through the village of Albrighton.

Your route joins the A528 at Harmer Hill. Continue into Shrewsbury. Entering Shrewsbury centre from the roundabout continue straight into the centre along by the river. Follow signs to Oswestry A5 then go downhill and follow signs to all routes A49. At a large roundabout follow Ludlow A49 off to your right. Go straight across three more roundabouts following Ludlow. At the next round-about follow Leominster. This is a busy roundabout crossing the main A5 road. Walk over Bayston Hill. This is a particularly busy section so take care.

Continue on the A49 towards Ludlow and Leominster. Go through the villages of Dorrington then Leebotwood. There is a footpath in parts of this section. Walking along the foot of the hills on your left, the scenery is quite outstanding. Turn off on the B4365 at the entrance to Church Stretton then onto the B4371 to Much Wenlock at the lights. Turn off again a short distance after to Hope Bowdler then to Studley and Ticklerton on a minor road. Walk on this winding lane to a T-junction at Ticklerton. Turn right then second left to Westhope. The roads here are narrow, picturesque and tree lined.

Descending to Westhope continue through the village towards the B4368 to Seifton. At a T-junction turn right then left after 100 yards towards Seifton. There is no signpost so refer to your map here. At another T-junction turn right into Seifton. You reach Culmington where the road passes over Ludlow racecourse. Rejoin the A49 here and turn left towards Leominster.

Plate 8
Entering Hereford centre just before the racecourse.

Plate 9
The short ascent before descending into Monmouth.

Turn left again on the B4361 to Ludlow. There are a lot of B&B's in this area. Keep on the main B4361 through Ludlow. Ascend the hill then descend to the traffic lights. Walk over the bridge ascending out of the town on the B4361 to Richards Castle, following the B4361 to Leominster.

Arriving at a T-junction on a bend go across towards Brecon A44. Walk through Leominster town centre then follow A49 sign to Hereford at a mini roundabout. There are a number of B&B's here. Go through Wharton village on the B4361. Walking to a roundabout rejoin the A49 to Hereford. Stay on the A49 passing Queenswood Country Park then descending to Wellington. Pass through Moreton on Lugg. Walk into Hereford (plate 8) passing the racecourse on your right and retail park on your left. At the mini roundabout follow Ross A49 sign to your left. At the next mini roundabout turn right following Ross on Wye A49. Pass Hereford United football club on your left. Follow the road to Ross then Monmouth. The road by-passes Hereford town centre going over the river Wye. At a roundabout turn left on the A49 Ross/Monmouth. Arriving at traffic lights go straight across going out of town on a slight ascent. There are a number of farms and houses offering B&B here. There are no footpaths after leaving Hereford but you can walk on the grass along the A49. Ascend the hill 3 miles out of Hereford then turn off on the A466 leading directly to Monmouth. You pick this road up 1 mile from the top of the hill clearly signposted Monmouth A466. It is an undulating road but away from the main traffic.

Walk through the village of Wormelow. At a fork in the road follow Monmouth off to your left. Pass through St. Weonards. Just before Monmouth go up a hill for 0.75 of a mile then downhill to Monmouth (plate 9). When you get to the T-junction at the traffic lights walk through Monmouth high street in a direct line through the town. Go over the bridge across the river, (plate 10) turn left then right onto the B4293 which goes to Trelleck in the Wye Valley. There is a good campsite in Monmouth near the fire station.

There is a 1 mile ascent out of Monmouth as you go over the A40. Walk through Trelleck and you should see a sign to Llandogo. Take that road then follow the next sign to Parkhouse off to your right. Keep on this narrow country lane to Parkhouse. There is a long downhill section going towards the A466. Near the bottom of the hill follow the sign to Tintern. Go over a bridge and through Tintern village.

After returning to the A466 turn right to Chepstow. Tintern Abbey is on your left. There are no footpaths in this area to walk on. Go through St. Arvans village. You walk past Chepstow racecourse. Follow Newport/Bristol M48 sign just after the racecourse at the roundabout. This takes you to the road over the Severn Bridge. Follow the sign to the Severn Bridge walking on the cyclist path on the right side. The views here are excellent. There is no charge for crossing the bridge in the easterly direction. On the east side of the bridge is Granada services (plate 11).

Plate 10

The gateway over the river to Monmouth town centre (south side).

Plate 11

The view from the bridge leading to the services at the East side of the Severn Bridge.
Your route looking West is on the left side of the road.

Once you have crossed the bridge a sign states Aust public footpath ½ mile. Follow this route unless you are crossing the motorway to the services. You will pass the Severn Bridge maintenance unit and straight onto the A403. Walk on this road to a sign to Pilning which is a minor road off to your left. Continue to a sign for Northwick which takes you down to Pilning then onto the A4055.

You pass over the M4 and on towards junction 17 of the M5. Turn left at a pub called the Cross Hands at a junction in Pilning. Walk through the village of Easter Compton, stay on this road going up the hill towards junction17 of the M5. Look for the A4018 Bristol west. Walk across a set of lights. At a roundabout turn left and walk past Clifton rugby ground. Turn right at another roundabout onto the A370.

Walk past Henbury swimming pool which is on your right and turn left at the next junction. Your route is signposted A38 Bridgewater. Follow sign to the West. You go through an open park area which is on both sides of the road. Go straight across two roundabouts. On a one way system follow south west sign through a games/park area. You see a sign Bridgewater A38 follow this walking past Bristol Zoo.

At the next crossroads go straight across. You should see Clifton Suspension bridge above. Walk to a dual carriageway following signs to Taunton A38 now. Cross a small roundabout and pass a bus depot. Cross the next two roundabouts then turn right at the third roundabout. Go uphill following A38 Taunton. There is a grass area on both sides of the road and a good view of Clifton Suspension bridge to your right. At the next roundabout follow Taunton A38 passing a sign saying 'Welcome to North Somerset'.

You ascend slightly as you leave the Bristol area. Keep on the A38 to Taunton as you pass through some traffic lights. A footpath runs along the roads throughout the Bristol area. Walk through Potters Hill, then pass the Bristol Tavern and airport.

There is a campsite 1.5 miles past Bristol airport. There are no footpaths here so use the grass verge if possible. There are excellent views of the Mendip Hills in front, then to your left as you walk towards Bridgewater.

Stay on the A38 passing through some traffic lights and cross road junctions. Go through the village of Cross where there are B&B's available. You cross over the M5 motorway on the A38 with your route now signed Exeter A38. Arriving at Edithmead roundabout continue on the A38 to Taunton, passing campsites on route.

Plate 12
Walking along the A30 near Victoria in Cornwall. Keep to the side of the road, walk facing the traffic.

Plate 13

Approaching the roundabout in Penzance with St. Michaels Mount in the background.

Cross the next roundabout through the village of Highbridge where there are shops to replenish your food store. Stay on the A38 to Bridgewater crossing over three roundabouts. Cross the river Parrett then turn left at the traffic lights.

Walk over the Bridgewater and Taunton canal, then through the lights, still on the A38. Cross two roundabouts taking the Taunton road. Go through North Petherton. There is another campsite at Monkton Heathfield. Cross the canal and turn right on the A38 at a junction. A dual carriageway takes you into Taunton. Walk on the grass verge. Follow signs to the town centre. Walk straight through the centre to avoid going around the ring road rejoining the A38 on the other side. Cross a small roundabout then pass a pub called the Stone Gallows which is recommended.

You walk through the village of Rummell with the Rummell Inn on your right. A footpath runs through this section. You walk past a cider farm and museum on your left. Follow signs to Exeter A38 and Tiverton at the next two roundabouts. You pass the sign for Devon and go through the Maiden Down. Cross over the M5 again and go through Waterloo Cross. Walk onto the A361 towards Tiverton after crossing over the M5 roundabout. Walk on the grass verge along this dual carriageway. Turn off on the A3391 towards Tiverton town centre. Go up the slip road then turn left at a small round-about towards the town centre.

Cross one small roundabout then right at the next. Take the Crediton A3072 road at the next roundabout. Walk over the next roundabout following Crediton signs. Cross a river then turn left at the next roundabout to Crediton. Cross another roundabout passing the Trout Inn on your right. Turn right, still on the A3072, just past the pub. Go over a small bridge look for Crediton signs.

There are good views of the Devon countryside from higher ground. Go through the village of Cadbury passing a sign for Cadbury Castle on the left. Take a long downhill walk, still on the A3072. You enter Crediton passing the Crediton Inn on your left. Turn right following Barnstable A377 ascending out of Crediton centre, then pass Crediton hospital as you leave the town. Look for a sign Knowle and Coleford to your left. Do not take the turning marked Knowle ½ mile.

In Coleford go across the crossroads ascending towards Bow. At the next main junction turn left back onto the A3072 towards Okehampton. This road leads onto the B3215 to Okehampton. Walk past the Countryman pub as you enter Okehampton. Descend a hill then follow Exeter A30 for a short distance. Arriving at some traffic lights turn right on the A30 towards Launceston. Walk through the centre of Okehampton staying on the A30. After 3 miles your road turns to dual carriageway. Walk along the side with care.

Plate 14
The final slight decent to Lands End.

Plate 15
Arriving at Lands End, your expedition complete.

Walking over Liftondown stay on the dual carriageway, do not go into Launceston. Now you enter Cornwall following the signs for Bodmin and walking over Bodmin Moor. Turn off to Bodmin on the A389. Walk to the bottom of the hill before turning right into Bodmin centre. Follow the road through the town following the sign for Redruth A38. Walk along Westheath Avenue as you leave Bodmin. Stay on the A389 until you meet the A30 again. Arriving at the roundabout rejoin the A30 by turning right. There are at least three campsites near here as you walk towards Lands End.

Pass the Victoria Inn on your left in the area known as Victoria. A railway runs parallel with the road. Continue on the A30 to Redruth (plate 12). You can see the sea on your right and soon after on your left. There are some electricity wind farms around here. Walk towards Redruth then Penzance on the A30. You may see a monument on a hill to your left in the distance as you pass Redruth. Stay on the A30 right to Lands End. In parts the road is two way.

Arriving at the roundabout at Hayle follow the sign to Penzance. Follow the sign to St. Ives at the next roundabout. You come to Canonstown still on the A30. There are footpaths or cycle routes on parts of the A30 you can use. Walk through Crowlas and as you near Penzance you should see St. Michael's Mount on your left (plate 13).

Your route leads towards the sea and a roundabout followed by another, still on the A30. Walk to Trianmore roundabout and follow signs to Lands End. Walk on paths then grass verge if necessary. Cross over a number of roundabouts but follow Lands End signs. Leaving Penzance a sign states Lands End 9 miles. Walk through the villages of Drift and Catchall. There are a number of caravan and campsites along the A30. A youth hostel is available 3 miles from the finish and a campsite 0.5 of a mile from Lands End.

The sea is on either side as you walk towards Sennen village just before Lands End. There is a car park a short distance from Lands End. You can see the end in sight now as you take the gentle walk to the finish line (plate 14).

Arriving at the gate of the Lands End complex (plate 15) the view all round is good, with the sea surrounding Lands End on 3 sides. Walk into the complex and register your successful completion in the 'Hall of Fame'. Your expedition is finally completed.

CONGRATULATIONS.

Post Walk

Once you have arrived at Lands End you should gain free access into the complex along with your support team if you have one. Visit the Hall of Fame at Lands End and take your form to be stamped and details recorded. You can purchase an official certificate here. After leaving the Hall of Fame go to the signpost for the official Lands End photos for your album. At Lands End there is a hotel on the site and food can be bought in the complex.

Outside of the complex there are youth hostels, B&B's and campsites available only a few miles up the road. The nearest main town is Penzance which is 11 miles from Lands End. Transport links to all parts of the country are situated here.

Your expedition is over and you can look forward to a well earned rest!

Appendix

i. Distances Between Prominent Landmarks

		miles
John O'Groats		
to		
Freswick	→	3
to		
Auckengill	→	3.8
to		
Keiss	→	2.6
Reiss		4.8
Wick		2.9
Thrumster		4.7
Latheronwheel		14.2
Dunbeath		2.6
Berriedale		6.8
Helmsdale		9
to		
Brora Village (south end)	→	12.3
to		
Golspie	→	4.7
Dornoch Firth Bridge		12.1
A9 Alness		15.2
Cromarty Firth Bridge		4.6
Tore		5.6
Inverness Roundabout		7.6
Tomatin Services		16.3
Aviemore (junction north)		13.8
Newtonmore (junction north)		13.8

Dalwhinnie (junction south)		16.7
Drumochter Summit		4.5
A9 Turn off towards Trinafour		6.7
to		
Trinafour	→	4.8
to		
Loch Kinardochy	→	10.2
to		
Kenmore	→	9.7
to		
Amulree	→	12.1
to		
Crieff	→	12.1
Braco		10.8
Dunblane south		8.6
Cumbernauld		18.5
Airdrie		5.3
Carluke		12.7
Lanark		5.5
A74 Abington		17.8
Crawford		3.6
Ecclefechan		41.6
Kirkpatrick Fleming		7.3
Gretna		4.5
Longtown		3.6
Carlisle		8.8
to		
J42 of M6	→	4.3
to		
Hackthorpe	→	21.6
to		
Shap	→	5.3

Kendal		15.7
Holme Burton		7.9
Carnforth		3.9
Lancaster		5.3
Barton		17.8
Preston		3.4
Euxton		5.1
Standish Village		9.3
Wigan		3.1
M6 Roundabout J23		7.8
Warrington		2.6
to		
Stockton Heath	→	6.3
to		
Whitchurch south	→	34.2
to		
Wem	→	8.5
to		
Shrewsbury	→	12.8
Dorrington		7.5
Culmington		18.6
Leominster		12.8
Hereford		12.6
Monmouth		20.8
Trellech		5.6
Tintern Abbey		5.9
Severn Bridge south		7.7
Bristol Airport		19.6
Cross Village		10.6
North Petherton		19.6

Waterloo Cross		24.6
to		
Tiverton Centre	→	5.9
to		
Crediton	→	14.6
to		
Okehampton	→	21.9
Bodmin		40
Victoria		8.6
Redruth A30		24.9
Hayle		6.4
Penzance		8
to		
Drift	→	3.5
to		
Lands End	→	7.6

Total Mileage   868.0

To find a distance read down then right e.g.
Bodmin to Victoria = 8.6 miles

ii. Tourist Information Centres on Route

Scottish Tourist Board	0131 332 2433
John O'Groats	01955 611373
Wick	01955 602596
Helmsdale	01431 821640
Dornoch	01862 810400
Inverness	01463 234353
Daviot Wood	01463 772203
Aviemore	01479 810363
Kingussie	01540 661297
Crieff	01764 652578
Dunblane	01786 824428
Stirling	01786 475019
Moffat	01683 220620
Gretna Green	01461 337834
Carlisle	01228 512444
Penrith	01768 867466
Kendal	01539 725758
Preston	01772 253731
Wigan	01942 825677
Warrington	01925 442180
Whitchurch	01948 664577
Shrewsbury	01743 350761
Ludlow	01584 875053
Hereford	01432 268430
Coleford	01594 836307
Bristol	0117 9260767
Bridgewater	01278 427652
Taunton	01823 336344
Tiverton	01884 255827
Crediton	01363 772006
Okehampton	01837 55611
Launceston	01566 772321
Bodmin	01208 76616
Penzance	01736 362207

iii. Campsites on Route

John O'Groats Camping Site	01955 611329
Dornoch Camping Park (2 miles off main road)	01862 810423
Daviot - Auchnahillin Camping Centre	01463 772286
Glenmore - Camping	01479 861271
Stirling - Auchenbowie Caravan Site	01324 822141
Moffat	01683 220436
Lockerbie	01387 810630
Gretna - The Braids	01461 337409
Carlisle - Dandy Dinmont Camping Park	01228 74611
Penrith - Lowther Caravan Park	01768 863631
Kendal - Millcrest	01203 694995
Lancaster - Venture Caravan Park	01524 412986
Garstang - Claylands Caravan Park	01524 791242
Wem - Lower Lacon Caravan Park (1.5 miles from town centre)	01939 232376
Shrewsbury - Beaconsfield Farm Caravan Park (2 miles north of Shrewsbury)	01939 210370
Hereford - Racecourse Campsite	01432 272364
Monmouth - Caravan Park	01600 714745

Hereford - Racecourse Campsite	01432 272364
Monmouth - Caravan Park	01600 714745
Chepstow - St. Pierre Campsite	01291 425114
Redhill - Brook Lodge Farm	01934 862311
Highbridge - New House Camping Park	01278 782218
Tiverton - Creacombe Parsonage Farm	01884 881441
Crediton	01363 772749
Okehampton - Moorcroft Leisure Park	01837 55116
Bolventor - Colliford Tavern Campsite	01208 821335
Indian Queens - Touring Park	01726 860812
Blackwater - Chiverton Touring Park	01872 560667
Hayle - St. Ives Holiday Park	01736 752274
Penzance - Bone Valley Holiday Park	01736 360313

iv. B&B's on Route

John O'Groats	House Hotel	01955 611203
	Mrs. Sinclair	01955 611297
Wick	Mrs. Green	01955 602076
	Mrs. Gunn	01955 603363
Helmsdale	The Old Manse	01431 821597
Brora	John Clarkson	01408 621332
Alness	Mrs. Jack	01349 884325
	Mrs. MacDougall	01349 882392
Inverness	Abb Cottage	01463 233486
	Mrs. Aird	01463 239338
Daviot	M. MacLeod	01463 772239
Aviemore	Mrs. Shaw	01479 811436
Kincraig	Mrs. MacLeod	01540 651313
Kingussie	Mr. Johnstone	01540 661052
Crieff	Ann Coutts	01764 653516
Bridge of Allan	Mr. Brown	01786 833018
Stirling	C. Cameron	01786 472681
Denny	Mrs. Russell	01324 812839
Moffat	Mrs. Jones	01683 220658
Lockerbie	Tarras Guest House	01576 203849

Gretna Green	Greenlaw Guest House	01461 338361
Carlisle	Kates Guest House	01228 539577
Kendal	Magic Hills House	01539 736248
Preston	Highland House	01772 861953
Warrington	The Hollies	01925 635416
Whitchurch	Pheasant Walk	01948 667118
Shrewsbury	Grove Farm	01939 220223
Dorrington	Ashton Lees	01743 718378
Hereford	Ashgrove House	01432 830608
Bridgewater	Admirals Rest	01278 458581
Taunton	Heathcroft	01823 275516
Tiverton	Lodge Hill Guest House	01884 252907
Crediton	Libbetts Cottage	01363 772709
Okehampton	Tawside House	01837 840183
Launceston	Mrs. Tucker	01566 775810
Penzance	Poniou Farm House	01736 366001

You may find throughout the summer months and particularly at peak holiday times, both campsites and B&B's do get booked up, so plan one or two days ahead and book in advance. Midweek should not be too much of a problem. One further point to be aware of is the prices which can be expensive both for camping and B&B's at peak times. Use your bivi bag if necessary on route.

v. Recommended Maps

Ordnance Survey Travelmaster 2
                    Northern Scotland
Ordnance Survey Travelmaster 4
                    Central Scotland
Ordnance Survey Travelmaster 5
                    Northern England
Ordnance Survey Travelmaster 7
                    Wales & West Midlands
Ordnance Survey Travelmaster 8
                    Southwest England

All maps to 1:250 000 scale or 1 inch to 4 mile

vi. Main Towns / Villages on Route

John O'Groats
Wick
Helmsdale
Brora
Golspie
Inverness
Daviot
Aviemore
Kingussie
Dalwhinnie
Crieff
Dunblane
Stirling
Denny
Cumbernauld
Airdrie
Lockerbie
Gretna Green
Carlisle
Penrith
Kendal
Lancaster
Preston
Wigan
Warrington
Weaverham

Whitchurch
Wem
Shrewsbury
Ticklerton
Ludlow
Leominster
Hereford
Monmouth
Chepstow
Severn Bridge
Bristol
Bishopsworth
Rooks Bridge
Bridgewater
Taunton
Tiverton
Crediton
Okehampton
Launceston
Bolventor
Bodmin
Redruth
Hayle
Penzance
Lands End

vii. Good Views on Route

John O'Groats
Duncansby Stacks
Northlands Viking Centre
Sinclair Bay
Wick - Caithness Glass
Dunbeath - Heritage Centre
Helmsdale - Timespan
Golspie - Dunrobin Castle
Dornoch Firth
Tain - Glenmorangie Distillery
Inverness - Moray Firth Bridge
Slochd Summit
Aviemore to Dalwhinnie
Glen Garry
Stirling
Carlisle Centre
Penrith to Kendal
Monmouth
Severn Bridge
Bristol Airport
Taunton
Okehampton
Bodmin Moor
Bodmin - Jamaica Inn
Launceston - Steam Railway
Redruth
Penzance - St. Michael's Mount
Lands End - Multiple Attractions

viii. Useful Addresses

Long Distance Walkers Association
Brian Smith
10 Temple Park Close, Leeds LS15 0JJ
Tel. 0113 264 2205
This association is set up to further the interests of those who enjoy long distance walking. Members receive a journal three times each year which includes information on all aspects of long distance walking.

Ramblers Association
1-5 Wandsworth Road, London SW8 2XX
Advice and information on all walking matters. Local groups with regular meetings.

Lands End - John O'Groats End to End Club
The Customs House, Lands End, Penzance, Cornwall TR19 7AA
Club co-ordinators Cilla George and John More
Tel. 01736 871501
Advice and information, route planning, magazines, special offers to club members.

Lands End Hotel Tel. 01736 871501
John O'Groats Hotel Tel. 01955 611203

The route described in this book was the one used by the author and believed to be correct at the time of publication. Over time roads/routes change and on this basis the author welcomes any information that would assist in keeping the book up to date.

Please write to :-

Challenge Publications
P.O. Box 132
Barnsley
S71 5YX